T0353907

CORKED

Diane Robitelle

Balboa Press books may be ordered through booksellers or by contacting:

Balboa Press
A Division of Hay House
1663 Liberty Drive
Bloomington, IN 47403
www.balboapress.com
844-682-1282

Because of the dynamic nature of the Internet, any web addresses or links contained in this book may have changed since publication and may no longer be valid. The views expressed in this work are solely those of the author and do not necessarily reflect the views of the publisher, and the publisher hereby disclaims any responsibility for them.

Any people depicted in stock imagery provided by Getty Images are models, and such images are being used for illustrative purposes only.
Certain stock imagery © Getty Images.

Interior Image Credit: Diane Carol Robitelle

ISBN: 979-8-7652-5086-0 (sc)
ISBN: 979-8-7652-5087-7 (e)

Library of Congress Control Number: 2024906320

Print information available on the last page.

Balboa Press rev. date: 05/24/2024

BALBOA.PRESS
A DIVISION OF HAY HOUSE

CONTENTS

I

H
E
A
R
I
N
G

Is there
anything
or anyone
un*marked* in life?
Do not our actions
our feelings and thoughts
make a *mark*
within ourselves,
upon others
and the world?
Do we not deliver
the past into the present?
Is anything ever fully gone
or forever forgotten?

UnMARKED ?

We leave our *stamp*
upon the envelope of space,
upon the stationary of time
with words, deeds
thoughts and feelings.

*M*ark
my
words!

2

ROADSIDE *ATTRACTIONS*

I ride on *to lasso*
enticing scenes,
spurred on
by roadside attractions.

I rope down *ideas,*
coil around *words,*
pull in *meaning*
like roped steers
pulled *to the ground.*

I *draw* down
sentences with
pencil on paper.

Now these *roped-in words*
wait to be *unbound,*
to be *read*   to *resound*
to l i v e a g a i n
to *roam the range.*

LAUNCH

Launch your words

matched to supersonic ideas

ignited with love

for the truth.

Let them soar

let them orbit the earth

and glow in her galaxy

then fall like shooting stars

full of meteoric iron

to infuse you

with strengthened will

for frequent flights.

Hearing **Here**
and *Beyond*

Barges of words
drift down hallways,
carry around curves.

Muffled meanings meander,
memories float past
flowing into present.

Their sounds sing
in listening hearts,
kind words uplift
for what fell apart

when we stopped

listening beyond hallways,
across unseen boundaries
where ideas live,
where meaning is found.

What's
In
Words

You speak   I listen
               yet what
               you are
               saying
               is not
               said
I hear   You speak
          the
          intention   g
          and the   n
          unintended   i
                    n
               a
          e   louder
     M   *s p e a k s*
                         than *words*

6

COULD

HAVE   *If what had happened*

  BEEN   had not happened

                  it could *have been* different.

                If what was learned

           had not been taught

          If what was heard

        had not been said

      If what was grown

     had not been planted

  it could *have been* different.

  What *could have been done*

    when *wrong*

                was not right

      when *sorrow*

                was not joy

      when *weak*

                was not strong

        it could *have been* different.

7

THE SOUND
of
WAITING

Listen to it   that *sound* of   WAIT ___
it's packed full of potential
full of possibilities
positioned for surprises
in future unfoldings

But WAIT ___
more is in the wings   set off stage
the past is always there
waiting ___ to enter center stage   to play
its memorized part in the present

But WAIT ___
when the playwright watches
from the audience   seeing
the real role of the past
the script can be changed
for the present to play out differently
and create new possibilities
for the future   just WAIT ___

Tune-up, listen in stillness, find concert pitch pulling together orchestra members as one body sounding individual tones, ready to play the 9th Symphony written and later conducted by Beethoven. *Though deaf to outer sound his inner world was alive with music.*

S   *After the conducting* stopped
           with **baton held high,**
Y   **nobody moved.**

M   *After the tones* **sounded,**
           all held still,
P   **no silence broken.**

H   *Aftertones* **lingered,**
           bathed in quiet,
O   **no bubbles burst.**

N   *Only sounds of* **silence**
           filled the space,
Y   **no audience angst.**

Sips of resounding tones
filled within, to the brim,

no spilled 'Ode to Joy'.

MORE

Is there *more* to say,
what was heard,
what is to be said?

W

   A

     I

       T

Know when
the time is right
for speaking
life-giving thoughts,
feeling their vitality,
courage and tranquility
for speaking words
worded to serve
the world.

II

FEELING

House Building

How do we view our life within ?

Today __ did we create goodwill,

did we think life-giving thoughts,

did we feel joy of life and fiery courage

with peaceful flow and breath of well-being ?

How do we view life from behind our door ?

Today __ did we sit inside ourselves

with cold thoughts and hard feelings

piled high against different people ?

How do we view life through our window ?

Today __ were we aware of the wolf

howling around the house with its

cold, brick-hard thoughts and feelings ?

How do we view life in our living room ?

Today __ did we see inside ourselves then

create warm thoughts and gentle feelings

toward different people ?

How did we build our house today ?

Who Goes There?

Go I ~ feeling
dark as a moonless night
bright as a sunny day
a color-filled soul
to bridge the storm-swept sky.

Go I ~ thinking
dark of doubt
light of certainty
colourful purpose
to bridge the gap to knowing.

Go I ~ willing
to know darknesses
to shine light
to bridge earth to heaven
heaven to earth.

SEEING with SOUL

Like the unseen wind
unseen thoughts breeze by
leaving traces

Like the unseen wind
unseen feelings waft away
leaving marks

Like the unseen wind
unseen deeds die down
leaving memories

of what has gone on
and glimpses
of what will go on

like the unseen wind

What's
in a
Name

Melissa------
it must mean
honey-mead - an elixir - a divine potion
given freely to friend or foe

Surely, she shall secure sensible signs
amongst the menacing multitude,
wherever she goes

goodness passes with her

She spins straw into gold,
the broken dried-up words
whispered to her become
wholecloth woven with

light of understanding

This communion
fills each cup
with the elixir of life,
quenching the thirst
of the multitude.

HIM
and
        HER

'**Where are you?**', she **shouted, 'I can't see you!'**
Where did he go? Was he hiding
from her or from himself?

He had painted his own inner canvas with a false face,
the one he chose to exhibit.
He questioned if it was time
to show his true colors beneath his facade
as he slunk around the Picasso room.

She stalked down the gallery hallway
then entered the room of the artist Van Gogh,
She stopped in front of his portrait,
the one showing his missing ear.

Why had he chosen this painting to exhibit?
Was he also saying he didn't want to hear
or he was not heard?

She then turned within herself
to see what she had painted
on her own inner canvas.

DARK
WATERS

We're drowning in bottles __
bottles
bottles of bottled-up anxiety,
anxiety darkening the waters of life.

Drinking doesn't quench thirst __
thirst
thirst that cries for deep relief,
relief springing from self-dug wells.

Dig to the bottom of anxiety down __
down
down to bedrock foundation
where TRUTH lies
where we can stand.

We have bottled up depths __
depths
depths to plunge
plunge
plunge dark waters
waters
waters to cross __ to cross
toward
the light
of knowing of seeing
our true self.

LIFE RHYTHMS

Feeling *beats of* life *for life*

sensing *feeling's flow of* changes

circulating *currents of* caution

currents *of* courage

H E A R T

chambering delicate dancing
touching   spiraling   swirling

rhythms *of* life *like lively sea tides*

moving   in *and* out   out *and* in

waves of *sad +* joy *fear +* courage

waves of *hate +* love *doubt + certainty*

pulsing thru our ocean *of* Being

E

  T

S   E

T   R

A   N

N   A

C

E   **What**   L

is

it

saying

about

where

I AM ?

I

stand

amidst

clear flowing water

a rapid river running

through

behind _____ *in front*

*of **me***

I

look

downstream _____ *upstream*

feeling

refreshing

flow

away ___ *toward*

far _____ *near*

later _____ *now*

cold _____ *warm*

past _____ *present*

present

future

There's an owl in the moonlit sky tonight

with wings spread shadowing the earth

There's an owl calling through the night tonight

Who whooo WHO are you?

Its question flies into souls tonight

into souls seeking salvation

*W*HO?

There's an owl in the light blue sky today

with wings outspread hovering o're the earth

There's an owl calling through the day today

You youuu LIGHT are you!

Its answer flies into souls today

into souls finding salvation

III

REFLECTING

Is life *like moving* on the treadmill
going   going
going somewhere   going nowhere
over and over?
Yet __ we're on-the-go   *making the best of it.*
This is as good as it gets.

Years piling up with stuff
attics packed   closets cluttered   basements bulging
no space to move
feeling stuffed   squeezed   boxed-in.

Is living *like riding* on a Ferris wheel
'round and 'round
'round highs   'round lows
over and over?
Yet __ we're on-the-move   *making the best of it.*
This is the way it is!

Yet ____ is this *all* there is?

        Is there a place
            beyond duties   beyond routine?
    Is there a bigger space
        beyond boxes   beyond square-corner rooms?
    Is there a bigger view
        beyond reach of hand   beyond sight of eyes?

IS THERE ?

Mail of junk
is mail of armour
all that junk
clogging boxes
with
    yes clutter
    yes chatter
    yes clink
    of death.

JUNK
MAIL

Mail of junk
is mind of metal
all that junk
boxed-in
with
    no art
    no music
    no poetry
of life.

On the brink

standing on the edge   looking down
pondering the plunge   but
paralyzing thought freezes movement
when looking at the long way
            down
            down
                down to deep water

water   once as icebound as
immobilized thought
until the sun shines down
creating cracks   making melt   letting life flow

will I die in frozen motion   or
let life flow here on the brink?
I tell myself to change focus:
                think   thoughts creating courage
                think   love for leaping   into
                    breath of air   world of water

think   I can   I will
step calmly from the edge
knowing my true self
            feeling the air

                    like a p a r a c h u t e
                        and
                        jump
                        into
                        the
                        meaning
                        of
                        life

Cut *the* Knot

Days of darkness, caught in its clutches,
seems forever   all is knot.
All there is   is too dark, with dark, for dark.
See it, name it, say it.
Recall Self *with light*
            to light
                for light.

Climb out of black crude remains,
arise from pits of past patterns.
Pivot to present life,
create Self *for future sustainability.*

Only what's true, good, beautiful
enlivens, enkindles, evolves the world.
Die to knotted threads of thinking,
birth a new Self   moment to moment
                year to year
                    lifetime to lifetime.

pieces
                        to PEACE

When poisonous powerplay is the game,
grabbing from others   for personal gain,
gaining power property and wealth,
then powerful personalities tightly grip,
tightly hold on to their pieces.

Hold on   wait up work for inner freedom,
learn selfless love to love others.
Level the playing field make PEACE.

No one is left out
when human value is the call.
No one is threatened
when respectful truth is the rule.
 No one is struck out
  when goodwill goes over the wall.

When PEACE is the name of the game,
making space for *everyone* to gain
the *unifying ideal*
then moral power of our true self
can take hold of the whole
to move from *pieces*
                        to PEACE.

What Time Is It?

It's time ___
time to *comb out snarls of the day*
time to *untangle strands of confused conversation*
time to *make straight all knotted ways.*

It's time ___
time to *brush away stray thoughts at night*
time to *settle down feelings of unrest*
time to *smooth out rhythms within.*

It's time ___
time to *wash from top to bottom*
time to *disinfect soreness of wounds*
time to *make clean all ways of the soul.*

It's time ___
time to *bed down to unwind events*
time to *calmly recall what was*
time to *get a new view of oneself*
       to see
        the self
         as a stranger
          at a clear distance ___ undisturbed.

B O D Y *LANGUAGE*

The body is like a mystery book
                                      read to know whodunit
The body is like a poet's paper
                                      words make marks
The body is like a teacher's slate
                                      instructions come and go
The body is like a loyal friend
                                      taking in thoughts and feelings
The body is like a musician's song
                                      tone tells feelings
The body is like a potter's clay
                                      movements make impressions
The body is like a painter's canvas
                                      images spark moods
The body is like a dancer's steps
                                      patterns are repeated
The body is like an actor's script
                                      episodes reveal changes
The body is like a storyteller's tale
                                      events leave effects

THIRTY-THREE

My eyes opened seeing
touching   grasping
not the same large window
not the same long curtain

for I saw anew
on the morning I awoke
finding the large window
with long curtain
aglow with the sun.

That morning I saw
        not only the glowing
                red of seamless cloth
I saw a dark shape cast upon it
    a striking shadow
        of the pane's two cross pieces.

That morning marked
thirty-three years on earth
when I died
to the thought

'I bear the cross'

and gave birth

to the thought

'The cross carries me'.

SO, *THE STORY GOES*

On her deathbed, grandmother opened her purse,
pulled out dollar bills, threw them in the air __
crying, "Poo, what good is money!"

So, *the story goes*
On her rough road, mother opened her savings,
put hard-earned money into meaningful projects __
seeing, what was worth supporting.

So, *the story goes on*
Along her working way, daughter opens her wallet,
pulls out paychecks, clutched in fist __
swearing, "Money is for purchasing products, not people!"

So, *the story goes on and on*
Along her path, grandaughter opens her pack,
discovers work has value when serving needs of others __
learning, wages cover living costs, but freedom is earned.

So, *the story goes far*
On her quest, great grandaughter opens her safe,
unlocked when turning away from greedy self-wealth __
prospering, working for others, living selfless ideals.

So, *the story goes further*
On her day of birth, great-great-grandaughter opens herself,
finds earthly ways within mother's embrace __
breathing, "I am one with the world."

IV

UNIFYING

Child

Oh child *when you wake*
stand   down on solid ground ~
touch firm support
sense deep depths below
dark dense earth underfoot.

Oh child *when you play*
feel   widening widths around ~
breathe nature's beauty
its carousel of colours   countless forms
curious tones   captivating movements.

Oh child *when you sleep*
see   night open its umbrella heights ~
soar to shining showers of stars
dip in pools of pure light
bathe in quiet rest above.

ARISE

So, **from seed-ground below**
to flower-seed above ------
the way is slow to grow.

So, *like a rosebud, unfold*
out of the thorny twig,
bring beauty to the garden of life.

So, **germinate life-filled ideas,**
cultivate courage ------
the way is slow to change.

So, *like a rosebud, unfold*
out of the thorny twig,
bring beauty to the garden of life.

So, **arise with the light of thinking**
for fruitful deeds of love ------
the way is slow to perfection.

So, *like a rosebud, unfold,*
out of the thorny twig,
bring beauty to the garden of life.

Mineral, Plant, Animal and Human Kingdoms

Being human, we are the crown of creation
made responsible for further education.
Now we are to learn how to know what to do
or else our four kingdoms pay in tribulation.

Live into the world by which we are embraced,
what is the difference between the kingdoms we now faced;
we lovingly look and ponder what is there,
to know on what our judgements are based.

On *mineral* foundations we solidly stand,
sentient beings move in air, water, and land,
colourful *plant* growth gives life to the living
and *animal* nature *humans* learn to command.

What does it matter to consider such things;
knowing truth creates for us wings.
With heightened view relations are known:
Four kingdoms sound together as each uniquely sings.

COMMUNITY GARDEN

Sow seeds of thoughtful deeds,
    like expectant gardeners
    sowing summer crops,
    knowing life sprouts when well-tended.

Root truth, grow goodness,
    feel beauty blossom,
    knowing deeds of love and wisdom
    will bear future fruit.

Harvest nourishment
    when ripeness of time is fulfilled
    then a city of sowers can rejoice
    in becoming a flourishing community.

HARVESTING SUMMER

Where there was greening growth
now there is browning decay.
Where there were long days of light
now there are longer nights of dark.

Where then can
light and growth
be found?

Summer has given   her sungold
Autumn is a memory   of warm riches
a reminder of winter's   cold wake
a funeral of loss   yet   a celebration of life

when summer's
light and growth
is sought within.

Where there is *enlightened thinking*
then there is *warming feeling.*
Where there is *charged willing*
then seeds of soul are sown
for a future
harvesting
of words.

THE PROMISE

The long windrow acreage of grey cloud
hovers high over raked hayfields,
its swirling droplets, waters of life,
let go to thirsting land below.

Fresh light green springs up,
newness replacing old brown
lingering reminders of fall's harvest
before winter's claim on waiting seeds
holding the promise of future fulfillment.

We too thirst for waters of life as we follow seasons,
witnessing withering and dying, living and flourishing,
our inner life calls for renewal, cycles of change within,
holding the promise of future fulfillment.

Let go of the lower self to hover high in fields of knowledge
to replace thoughts that gather like grey clouds,
to silent feelings that swirl around like windswept rain,
when thirsting to know life-giving thoughts.

Season of the Long Shadows

It is the season of the long shadows
    marking the sun's passage
    with bright eye sighting low to earth
    with bare trees bowing black beams on white
    with soft snow seeping quiet into ground.

It is the season of the silent sundials
    marking the passage of time
    with short days of light
    with long nights of dark
    with freezing cold North winds.

It is the season of the inbreath
    marking the space
    with waiting seeds lying still
    with frozen ground grave quiet
    with silent buds wrapped tight.

It is the season of the indrawn
    marking the inner work
    with seeing the shadows
    with naming the darknesses
    with knowing the light of thinking.

It is the season of the dead
    marking the inner death
    with turning away from growth
    with lifeless ideas and fear
    with confusion and destruction.

It is the season of the birth
    marking the inner life
    with opening to grow
    with choosing loving thoughts for living
    with gaining wisdom to shape a true self.

Words of Water

sparkling snow cloaks
my still shoulders

clear ice covers
my quiet depths

etched lines crease
my frozen face

sharp blades carve
my deep secrets

as a silent skater considers
my winter water

wondering about
my   three   ways   of   being

solid ice   flowing water   rising vapor

then the skater sees human beings
their   three   ways   of   being

body solid   soul flowing   spirit r i s i n g

V

SEEING

REDWOODS

Blessed is silent slow growth
surrounding heart's core
bounded by dark furrowed bark,
holding layer upon layer of stories
ringing out cycles of seasons.

Blessed is deep down stillness
rooted in heart's core
built up from firm ground
climbing to towering tops
quietly revealing ancient runes.

Blessed is old growth
speaking to our heart's core
sounds of patience, sounds of peace
sheltering us with giant gestures,
embracing us with untouchable time.

Blessed is their quiet growing
sounding in me
their silence growing deeper
and I growing fuller
so the forest fills me
                and I fill the forest.

HEARTLAND

O p e n w i d e ___ like an Alberta sky
let light and shadow play
across the landscape of your soul
as grey clouds billowing by the sun
warn of rains to come

Now breathe in fertile fields
ripening a feeling for joy in growth
of life-giving grains
and blessings of oils
in sun-yellowing crops
to fill your cup
with overflowing goodness

Behold boundaries of trees and fences
between neighbours
who know where and when to cross

Find tranquility planted
like the shelter of trees
surrounding homesteads

Feel the pulse of prairie heartland
as you hover like a hawk on high
with a far-ranging view
in search of deep dwelling

T
R
U
T
H

MOCCASIN, MONTANA

Moccasin ___ made for walking
only a short walk from past to present
through this tiny town well trodden with a history.

Memories etched in empty
darkened house remains
scattered among the more modern.

Life and death cycles
under Big Sky stretching
over Montana's mileage.

Round hayrolls
bed down on flat land,
summer's wad wrapped for winter's feed.

Giant grain bins store life
gone from golden wheat stubble,
whiskers to the wind that chin up to change.

Well-worked land
is laid to rest
at harvest end.

FROM

    TOP   We refresh ourselves

    TO   in the midst of innocence

    BOTTOM   where rugged m o u n t a i n j a w s open

           with jagged teeth bared to catch

          whitest snow   life-giving rain   sunlight   air

     and wild winds blow across sharp edges

We drink-in these seasoned peaks

  downing one for the road

    as we drive away

      on paved tongue

        toward tunnel throat

         only to get swallowed

          again in hard to stomach

           greedy bowel

            of self-seeking city-life

travelers

snaking through **mountains**
mountains
with white cloud-caped shoulders
softening, soothing souls of tense travelers
traversing narrow passages of **dark**
dark
mounds of mother earth,
making way   to light-filled spaces,
places warmly welcoming **life**
life
swarming in honeycomb seaside cities
where travelers meet off busy streets
in places   humming with satisfied **sounds**
sounds
of friends sitting 'round tables, settling in
to eat, to drink, to clink stemmed glasses
glasses of grape wine   nectar of the gods,
sun-filled joy pouring out   raying into rooms,
spilling into **roadways**
roadways
cobbled together, connecting
place-to-place   person-to-person
this time   in **this space** .

now remembering past,
present in bulging brick walls
housing many generations over time.
now mis-matched   dis-placed,
destined for dis-order   in order to know
how   when   where to meet
this time   in **this place.**

45

BY *LAND SEA* and *AIR*

We do *fall,* **fall victim**
      to false propaganda
      to fear, hatred, doubt,
      with their war words shouting for security.

We do *fight,* **fight for secure lives**
      with bullets, bombs, blood let loose,
      with life lost, let go.

Do we *win,* **win security**
      with boots on the ground, ships over the sea,
      with fighting jets in the air?

Do we *conquer,* **conquer secure lives**
      with ammunitions
      with army, navy, airforce?

We do *kill,* **kill ourselves**
      with not conquering doubt, hatred, fear,
      with not battling those beasts within.

We do *rise,* **rise to realness**
      with life-giving light-filled ideas
      with love-filled moral deeds
      to truly become human.

Will we *find,* **find connections of our bone to land,**
      blood to sea and breath to air,
      to feel we live together in the worldwide-all?

Will we build, **build a world**
      of land sea and air
      to live in peace?

E   A   R   T   H   *2010 Earthquake in Haiti*

M

O   Heaps of crumbled chaos

V   piles of brokenness

E   layers of loss   *Earth moves*

S   *splits open*

                                     so do we

Feel pain panic sorrow despair
loosened from life as it was
spread like uncountable cracks
too wide to leap too deep to hide   *Earth moves*
                                           splits open
                                           so do we

Feel heaviness
broken   hearts   bones
lost lives limbs
shattered   hopes   homes   *Earth moves*
                                  splits open
                                  so do we

Feel moved to give
a helping hand
dig in pockets
through rumble
down deep to lives   *Earth moves*
                           splits open
                           so do we

Voices sound   THE GULF
  as sunlit air fills with gentle winds
   sweeping across waters washing life of shores
    while fishing folk haul shrimp, oysters, fish from the sea.

   Voices cry
    as blue sky fills with billows of black smoke
     exploding upward from oilrig fire
      fed by crude blasts coughed up from the deep.

    Voices call
     as darkened air fills with threatening winds
      sweeping across oily waters wasting life of shoals
       while fishing folk watch oil gush in the Gulf.

     Voices rise
      as dark grief fills with fear of future
       sweeping across oiled waters
        while fishing folk lose livelihood of the sea.

      From disaster it is time to turn the tide
       toward visioning, creating, living
        safer sustainable lives.

       Sound Cry Call Rise!
       Sound   sureness
        knowing what's true.
        Cry Call   concern
         feeling what's right.
         Rise   responsibly
          seeing what's good.

         Then oily waters, fires, deaths   end
          when greed, power, control   stop
           from creating   the   gulf.

VI

QUEST
T
I
O
N
ING

SIGN of the TIMES

Have you seen the sign
the church sign saying
free bread and wine?

Who has seen the sign
the sign saying
free yourself?

Be free from dwelling
only on body and blood,
be free from Mammon
from power driven wealth.

Since signing off from the
Tree of Life   Tree of Paradise,
we signed on to know the
Tree of Knowledge of Good and Evil.

Have we seen its sign?
Its sign says
free yourself.

Climb to see and know
climb to know and see
climb to be free.

YEAR of NEW

It is time to *renew*   to *resolve*   to *resist*!

It is time to *review* the old year, to reveal past,
            create present, prepare future
            before years pass by,
            before we pass away.

It is time to *renew* for creating years
            of clarity, community,
            well-being, joy and light
            overcoming the dark.

It is time to *resist* from making years
            with worries, woes,
            confusion, conflict and
            darknesses dousing the light.

It is time to *resolve* to align
            with light of truth, to attend
            to goodwill and beauty, to awaken
            to the working of darkness.

It is time to *create* thoughts, feelings, deeds
            pure, worthy, real, born of love,
            born of light, to shape a new year,
            a new self : enlivened, courageous,
            a new self : tranquil and strong.

It is time to renew   to resolve   to resist !

Holyday Cheer

Where is the cheer for the Holydays
When wrong rings round the world
When battles blaze with gunfire
When cruel carnage claims lives?

What is the cheer for the Holydays
When right clangs against wrong
When war-wages wrap up wealth
When the gift of life loses meaning?

How is there cheer for the Holydays
When lies overshadow truth
When money-making means more than peace
When bodies are emptied of soul and spirit?

Why is there cheer for the Holydays
When false figures as fact
When power and greed run riot
When lives are lost in the dark?

Who is there to cheer the Holydays
When truth reigns as real
When loving deeds serve the world
When living creates light in the dark?

m u c h

o r

there is

too much

  too much   f e w

to gripe

groan

spit

bitch

cringe and cry

cry about

destroying!   are there

too few

too few

to grip

grow

  breathe

balance

  create and care

   care

      about evolving?

53

NIGHT VISION

The human race
can do more than
take a stab in the dark ,
at darkness blanketing
smothering and blocking
breaths of air .

The human race
    is on
        to conquer
            covid operations
                to clear the corona cover
                    surrounding the world .

The human race
can clear the way
with insight
piercing the dark .
Individuals can
spark to life
the light of thinking
for a night vision
that can
      see solutions .

Say What?

Did you say

we can't know?

Did you think thoughts

that set limits to knowing?

Think

there are no limits to knowing

for thought opens the way

to perceive universal truths

to do individual moral deeds

to feel one with the world!

Un*Knowable?*

I knew *I'd know*
but how did I know
I knew *I'd know?*

Since I knew *I'd know*
then somehow I must have known
how to know.

Now I know
an unknown
is an unknowable
only until I consciously know
how to know.

Now when I know
how to know,
I can truly know
what needs to be known

for the right deed
at the right time
in the right place.

VII

EX-
PLOR-
ING

THROUGH THE WORD

I felt
some
knowing
place ___
Words
weaving
you and me
together ___
Our strands
of sentences going
over and under
the other
crossing
meeting
in the midst
of movement ___
I found
some
knowing
place ___
Within
the words
was heard,
"I remember you!"

IN and OUT
the WINDOW

UNknowingly __ *from room to room*
she crossed thresholds
while seeking her way in the dark.

With no light of knowing shining forth
fear found her 'til un-coward by courage.

Slowly she moved
found a chair sat down
reached out
felt a curtain   opened it
faced a window   looked out.

She saw old friends lighting the night
pinpointing her place out and in the house.

Sparkling stars guiding to a heightened view
she found - the I AM - the light of knowing
shining in the dark.

So she readied herself
to cross thresholds
from earthlife to afterlife __ **knowingly.**

IN the
        BLINK
                of an EYE

There   and   gone
             are
bird flights   cloud forms

water waves   footprints

soul moods   and   memories

    as   time   turns

moving forward *and* bringing back

inner scenes   *and*   outer seasons

similar   yet   different

like the cycling of human lifetimes

BiRD'S EYE
V I E W

Years
have nested now
holding
heaps of happenings.

Each event
is yoked to me
even after
peeling out
of the white shell.

And I see a tapestry
woven with words
then weighed
by the feather
of truth.

P
  A
    S   **Thinking** *of you, friend,*
    S   with light of knowing
   I   **Feeling** *you, friend,*
 N   with warmth of love
G   **Willing** *you, friend,*
    fruitful harvesting from past deeds.

Now awaken   within starry realms
widen your reach   ever wider
moving through spheres of planets

Moon   Mercury   Venus
                Sun
  Mars   Jupiter   Saturn

Then when ready return
  with new deeds to sow
    for another fruitful harvest.

DEEP

SECRET

Shhhhh

I'll tell you a secret

I am ancient

lifetimes in the making

A long story

so long that I've forgotten

though I know

I was   I am   I will be

Shhhhhh

it's a secret

isn't it?

On *the Way*

Those telltale signs
  litter my inner being,
    my outer boundary
    just bordering on
      jump-out-of-my-skin,
        hop-over-the-fence
        excitement!

      I feel the edge of inevitable,
        the moment of miraculous,
          the cusp of change.

        I rejoice in the stream of life
          before and after birth,
            before and after death,
              spiralling *on the way* moving forward
                from what   to what   for what ?

          What were our beginnings
            that fired up our will to move on;
            what is the aim drawing us to the future;
          how do we get to the goal ?

        What thoughts will move us *on the way,*
        on the way from narrow to broad,
        move us from doubt to certainty,
      move us from hate to love,
      move us from fear to courage ?

    For insight -- be OPEN
  to grasp the facts.

64

VIII

DECLARING

HEAVY
TRAFFIC

Caution...

bad feelings are

accelerating

they ne**ed** to **STOP!**

Put your foot down
give yourself a **break**.

Idle a couple minutes
before you *GO!*

You're **go**ing
to **drive** yourself

C r a z y

crazy with **bad** feelings

racing around

*your **inner** city.*

```
                              R
                                A
                                  I
        Loads loaded              L
       riding night rails           I
        tracking  clacking           N
       long longing                   G
      long longing
     longing for termination
   determination for terminal
 terminal of destination              -

              ending railing    railing
                ending tankers of dark thoughts
              flatbeds of foul feelings
              boxcars of wrong words
            terminating
          terminating
        terminating
```

BACK PAIN

Too many critical thoughts
stacked-up like spinal vertebrae

Too weighty for the structure
it twists and turns

Too soon torqued tissues
turn scornful

Too late pleading pain proclaims
twisted thoughts of downfall

Too little uplifting ideas fill spaces
between hardened bony feelings

Never too late for fluid flowing
with life-giving thoughts

Never too soon to fill dying tissues
with life - love of form - for a supple spine

Always time to feel warmth and balance
between the heights and the depths

After all __
        these many moons of dark
        dark begins to phase to light
        light of the new moon shines
        shines to show the dark

After all **these** __
        many moons of despair, of destruction
        from loss of meaning, of self, of home
        now we gain truth and reconciliation,
        find forgivers, feel forgiveness

After all these years __
        we turn to face the sun
        sun of warming rays
        rays of truth, of goodness
        rays of growth

After all __
        we turn to home on the land
        home in humanity, in oneself
        in a place to care-give
        from a place to live and let live

AFTER

We have wound our way
to the breaking point ___
our bowl filled with
plague and pollution.

Pain presses open   our
cracks of error   our
false face with its
ill-logic and illusion.

WHEN *the* BOWL BREAKS

When spirits *harden*

nerves *shatter*

then hearts *hasten*

and souls *scream*
muscles cramp
and tendons tighten.

What held together
finally falls apart ___
the bowl breaks open
we must make a new start.

```
                    -       -    Who's best?
              -                  Begin
      C                            the competition.
      R                          Line up!
      I                            Here come
      T                              criticisms
      I                                comparisons
      C                                like racehorses
      A                                out of the gates!
      L
                                   They're fast
      R                            around the track
      A                            nosing toward
      C                            the finish.
      E
                                   The stakes are high,
                                 riders jockeying
         Was it a race worth running   for first place.
              when who wins,
                only loses?
```

CRITICAL RACE

Who's best? Begin the competition. Line up! Here come criticisms comparisons like racehorses out of the gates!

They're fast around the track nosing toward the finish.

The stakes are high, riders jockeying for first place.

Was it a race worth running when who wins, only loses?

WHO IS
WHO

I felt BLOCKED   imprisoned
closed off after your captive question.

Before you asked I felt free   open
within a space without walls.

Afterwards I wondered why I felt smalled
then knew it was you   not me.

I felt your feelings   your critical thoughts
then lost my certainty   my truth of self.

Now I'm aware I can feel your thoughts
now I will know who
               is who.

Me ____ You

I am me ___ you are you,
we're not one ___ we are two.
It's no bother ___ to make that line
between your space ___ and space of mine.

Within our bodies ___ we are two
until we meet in thought ___ that's true.
Together with understanding ___ we rise
by life-giving thoughts ___ uniting the wise.

Then back into body-self ___ we fall,
within our line ___ behind our wall.
Conflicts come ___ when here too long,
when you are right ___ and I am wrong.

L

  I

    N

      E

Sky   S

meets

Earth.

Two make a borderline of horizon.

I meet You.

Two

  cross

    a

      boundary

        line

          through

            understanding.

74

LIVING WORD

Oh, to know life
  as the poet knows it
    living into the word,
      turning unappetizing feats
        into poetic feasts,
          taming these raging beasts
            of fear, doubt, and mockery.

      Oo, to dine on the finest,
        the living word,
          turning away
            from beastly appetites
              that leave only crumbs
                of ruined dispositions.

        Ah, to awake
          to the royal highness
            after bending low
              over the beggar's bowl

DAWN

A keyhole of light
shines through
dawn's grey door.
She spreads her morning message
on wakers of the day
--- s o u n d i n g ---
the heart of this world
silently rhythms over all
rippling rays of life   rising
out of quiet night
out of silent sleep
on those who wake
to find   to see   to know
new meaning this day.

Then our questions arise
with the dawning sunlight
and stream out searching
searching for answers.

For those who search
to find   to think   to know
turn darkness
to dawn
of a new day.

Acknowledgements

I lived with these poems a long time, long enough to experience a soul-ripening process playing into making several word changes. Also along the way was generous help of kind friends of poetry to whom I give heartfelt gratitude: Emanuel Blosser, Kayleigh Cline, Max Vandersteen, Diana Zinter, Michael Lapointe, Carol Oczkowska. They read or reread the poems, giving editorial comments and kind encouragement, which provided progress toward the goal of offering well-aged words that now no longer need to be CORKED.

Printed in the United States
by Baker & Taylor Publisher Services